THE PLAYER QUEEN

By W. B. YEATS

A Digireads.com Book
Digireads.com Publishing

The Player Queen
By W. B. Yeats
ISBN 10: 1-4209-4169-0
ISBN 13: 978-1-4209-4169-2

Please visit *www.digireads.com*

PERSONS IN THE PLAY

DECIMA
SEPTIMUS
NONA
THE QUEEN
THE PRIME MINISTER
THE BISHOP
THE STAGE MANAGER
THE TAPSTER
AN OLD BEGGAR
OLD MEN, OLD WOMEN,
CITIZENS, COUNTRYMEN,
PLAYERS, etc.

SCENE I: *An open space at the meeting of three streets.*
SCENE II: *The Throne Room.*

SCENE I

An open space at the meeting of three streets. One can see for some way down one of these streets and at some little distance it turns, showing a bare piece of wall lighted by a hanging lamp. Against this lighted wall are silhouetted the heads and shoulders of two old men. They are leaning from the upper windows, one on either side of the street. They wear grotesque masks. A little to one side of the stage is a great stone for mounting a horse from. The houses have knockers.

FIRST OLD MAN. Can you see the Queen's castle? You have better sight than I.

SECOND OLD MAN. I can just see it rising over the tops of the houses yonder on its great rocky hill.

FIRST OLD MAN. Is the dawn breaking? Is it touching the tower?

SECOND OLD MAN. It is beginning to break upon the tower, but these narrow streets will be dark for a long while. [*A pause.*] Do you hear anything? You have better hearing than I.

FIRST OLD MAN. No, all is quiet.

SECOND OLD MAN. At least fifty passed by an hour since, a crowd of fifty men walking rapidly.

FIRST OLD MAN. Last night was very quiet, not a sound, not a breath.

SECOND OLD MAN. And not a thing to be seen till the tapster's old dog came down the street upon this very hour from Cooper Malachi's ash-pit.

FIRST OLD MAN. Hush, I hear feet, many feet. Perhaps they are coming this way. [*Pause.*] No, they are going the other way, they are gone now.

SECOND OLD MAN. The young are at some mischief, the young and the middle-aged.

FIRST OLD MAN. Why can't they stay in their beds, and they can sleep too seven hours, eight hours. I mind the time when I could sleep ten hours. They will know the value of sleep when they are near upon ninety years.

SECOND OLD MAN. They will never live so long. They have not the health and strength that we had. They wear themselves out. They are always in a passion about something or other.

FIRST OLD MAN. Hush! I hear a step now, and it is coming this way. We had best pull in our heads. The world has grown very wicked and there is no knowing what they might do to us or say to us.

SECOND OLD MAN. Yes, better shut the windows and pretend to be asleep.

[*They pull in their heads. One hears a knocker being struck in the distance, then a pause and a knocker is struck close at hand. Another pause and Septimus, a handsome man of thirty-Five, staggers on to the stage. He is very drunk.*]

SEPTIMUS. An uncharitable place, an unchristian place. [*He begins banging at a knocker.*] Open there, open there. I want to come in and sleep.

[*A third Old Man puts his head from an upper window.*]

THIRD OLD MAN. Who are you? What do you want?

SEPTIMUS. I am Septimus. I have a bad wife. I want to come in and sleep.

THIRD OLD MAN. You are drunk.

SEPTIMUS. Drunk! So would you be if you had as bad a wife.

THIRD OLD MAN. Go away.

[*He shuts the window.*]

SEPTIMUS. Is there not one Christian in this town. [*He begins hammering the knocker of the First Old Man, but there is no answer.*] No one there? All dead or drunk maybe bad wives. There must be one Christian man.

[*He hammers a knocker at the other side of the stage. An Old Woman puts her head out of the window above.*]

OLD WOMAN [*in a shrill voice*]. Who's there? What do you want? Has something happened?

SEPTIMUS. Yes, that's it. Something has happened. My wife has hid herself, has run away, or has drowned herself.
OLD WOMAN. What do I care about your wife! You are drunk.

SEPTIMUS. Not care about my wife! But I tell you that my wife has to play by order of the Prime Minister before all the people in the great hall of the Castle precisely at noon and she cannot be found.
OLD WOMAN. Go away, go away! I tell you, go away. [*She shuts the window.*]

SEPTIMUS. Treat Septimus, who has played before Kubla Khan, like this. Septimus, dramatist and poet! [*The Old Woman opens the window again and empties a jug of water over him.*] Water! drenched to the skin must sleep in the street. [*Lies down.*] Bad wife others have had bad wives, but others were not left to lie down in the open street under the stars, drenched with cold water, a whole jug of cold water, shivering in the pale light of the dawn, to be run over, to be trampled upon, to be eaten by dogs, and all because their wives have hidden themselves.

[*Enter two Men a little older than Septimus. They stand still and gaze into the sky.*]

FIRST MAN. Ah, my friend, the little fair-haired one is a minx.

SECOND MAN. Never trust fair hair I will have nothing but brown hair.

FIRST MAN. They have kept us too long brown or fair.

SECOND MAN. What are you staring at?

FIRST MAN. At the first streak of the dawn on the Castle tower.

SECOND MAN. I would not have my wife find out for the world.

SEPTIMUS. [*sitting up*] Carry me, support me, drag me, roll me, pull me, or sidle me along, but bring me where I may sleep in comfort. Bring me to a stable my Saviour was content with a stable.

FIRST MAN. Who are you? I don't know your face.

SEPTIMUS. I am Septimus, a player, a play-wright and the most famous poet in the world.

SECOND MAN. l hat name, sir, is unknown to me.

SEPTIMUS. Unknown?

SECOND MAN. But my name will not be unknown to you. I am called Peter of the Purple Pelican, after the best known of my poems, and my friend is called Happy Tom. He also is a poet.

SEPTIMUS. Bad, popular poets.

SECOND MAN. You would be a popular poet if you could.

SEPTIMUS. Bad, popular poets.

FIRST MAN. Lie where you are if you can't be civil.

SEPTIMUS. What do I care for any one now except Venus and Adonis and the other planets of heaven!

SECOND MAN. You can enjoy their company by yourself. [*The two Men go out.*]

SEPTIMUS. Robbed, so to speak; naked, so to speak bleeding, so to speak and they pass by on the other side of the street.

[*A crowd of Citizens and Countrymen enter. At first only a few, and then more and more till the stage is filled by an excited crowd.*]

FIRST CITIZEN. There is a man lying here.

SECOND CITIZEN. Roll him over.

FIRST CITIZEN. He is one of those players who are housed at the Castle. They arrived yesterday.

SECOND CITIZEN. Drunk, I suppose. He'll be killed or maimed by the first milk-cart.

THIRD CITIZEN. Better roll him into the corner. If we are in for a bloody day's business, there is no need for him to be killed an unnecessary death might bring a curse upon us.

FIRST CITIZEN. Give me a hand here.

[*They begin rolling Septimus.*]

SEPTIMUS. [*muttering*] Not allowed to sleep! Rolled off the street! Shoved into a stony place! Unchristian town!

[*He is left lying at the foot of the wall to one side of the stage.*]

THIRD CITIZEN. Are we all friends here, are we all agreed?

FIRST CITIZEN. These men are from the country. They came in last night. They know little of the business. They won't be against the people, but they want to know more.

FIRST COUNTRYMAN. Yes, that is it. We are with the people, but we want to know more.

SECOND COUNTRYMAN. We want to know all, but we are with the people.

[*Other voices take up the words, 'We want to know all, but we are with the people,' etc. There is a murmur of voices together.*]

THIRD CITIZEN. Have you ever seen the Queen, countryman?

FIRST COUNTRYMAN. No.

THIRD CITIZEN. Our Queen is a witch, a bad evil-living witch, and we will have her no longer for Queen.

THIRD COUNTRYMAN. I would be slow to believe her father's daughter a witch.

THIRD CITIZEN. Have you ever seen the Queen, countryman?

THIRD COUNTRYMAN. No.

THIRD CITIZEN. Nor has any one else. Not a man here has set eyes on her. For seven years she has been shut up in that great black house on the great rocky hill. From the day her father died she has been there with the doors shut on her, but we know now why she has hidden herself. She has no good companions in the dark night.

THIRD COUNTRYMAN. In my district they say that she is a holy woman and prays for us all.

THIRD CITIZEN. That story has been spread about by the Prime Minister. He has spies everywhere spreading stories. He is a crafty man.

FIRST COUNTRYMAN. It is true, they always deceive us country people. We are not educated like the people of the town.

A BIG COUNTRYMAN. The Bible says, Suffer not a witch to live. Last Candlemas twelve-month I strangled a witch with my own hands.

THIRD CITIZEN. When she is dead we will make the Prime Minister King.

SECOND CITIZEN. No, no, he is not a king's son.

SECOND COUNTRYMAN. I'd send a bellman through the world. There are many kings in Arabia, they say.

THIRD COUNTRYMAN. The people must be talking. If you and I were to hide ourselves, or to be someway hard to understand, maybe they would put some bad name on us. I am not against the people, but I want testimony.

THIRD CITIZEN. Come, Tapster, stand up there on the stone and tell what you know.

[*The Tapster climbs up on the mounting-stone.*]

TAPSTER. I live in the quarter where her Castle is. The garden of my house and the gardens of all the houses in my row run right up to the rocky hill that has her Castle on the top. There is a lad in my quarter that has a goat in his garden.

FIRST CITIZEN. That's strolling Michael—I know him.

TAPSTER. That goat is always going astray. Strolling Michael got out of his bed early one morning to go snaring birds, and nowhere could he see that goat. So he began climbing up the rock, and up and up he went, till he was close under the wall, and there he found the goat and it shaking and sweating as though something had scared it. Presently he heard a thing neigh like a horse, and after that a something like a white horse ran by, but it was no horse, but a unicorn. He had his pistol, for he had thought to bring down a rabbit, and seeing it rushing at him as he imagined, he fired at the unicorn. It vanished all in a moment, but there was blood on a great stone.

THIRD CITIZEN. Seeing what company she keeps in the small hours, what wonder that she never sets foot out of doors.

THIRD COUNTRYMAN. I Wouldn't believe all that night rambler says—boys are liars. All that we have against her for certain is that she won't put her foot out of doors. I knew a man once that when he was five and twenty refused to get out of his bed. He wasn't ill—no, not he, but he said life was a vale of tears, and for forty and four years till they carried him out to the churchyard he never left that bed. All tried him— parson tried him, priest tried him, doctor tried him, and all he'd say was, 'Life is a vale of tears.' It's too snug he was in his bed, and believe me, that ever since she has had no father to rout her out of a morning she has been in her bed, and small blame to her maybe.

THE BIG COUNTRYMAN. But that's the very sort that are witches. They know where to find their own friends in the lonely hours of the night. There was a witch in my own district that I strangled last Candlemas twelvemonth. She had an imp in the shape of a red cat, that sucked three drops of blood from her poll every night a little before the cock crew. It's with their blood they feed them; until they have been fed with the blood they are images and shadows; but when they have it drunk they can be for a while stronger than you or me.

THIRD COUNTRYMAN. The man I knew was no witch, he was no way active. ' Life is a vale of tears,' he said. Parson tried him, doctor tried him, priest tried him—but that was all he'd say.

FIRST CITIZEN. We'd have no man go beyond evidence and reason, but hear the Tapster out, and when you have you'll say that we cannot leave her alive this day— no, not for one day longer.

TAPSTER. It's not a story that I like to be telling, but you are all married men. Another night that boy climbed up after his goat and it was an hour earlier by his clock and no light in the sky, and when he came to the Castle wall he clambered along the wall among the rocks and bushes till he saw a light from a little window over his head. It was an old wall full of holes, where mortar had fallen out, and he climbed up, putting his toes into the holes, till he could look in through the window; and when he looked in, what did he see but the Queen.

FIRST COUNTRYMAN. And did he say what she was like?

THE TAPSTER. He saw more than that. He saw her coupling with a great white unicorn. [*Murmurs among the crowd.*]

SECOND COUNTRYMAN. I will not have the son of the unicorn to reign over us, although you will tell me he would be no more than half a unicorn.

FIRST COUNTRYMAN. I'll not go against the people, but I'd let her live if the Prime Minister promised to rout her out of bed in the morning and to set a guard to drive off the unicorn.

THE BIG COUNTRYMAN. I have strangled an old witch with these two hands, and to-day I will strangle a young witch.

SEPTIMUS. [*who has slowly got up and climbed up on to the mounting-stone which the Tapster has left*]. Did I hear somebody say that the unicorn is not chaste It is a most noble beast, a most religious beast. It has a milk-white skin and a milk-white horn, and milk-white hooves, but a mild blue eye, and it dances in the sun. I will have no one speak against it, not while I am still upon the earth. It is written in "The Great Beastery of Paris" that it is chaste, that it is the most chaste of all the beasts in the world.

THE BIG COUNTRYMAN. Pull him out of that, he's drunk.

SEPTIMUS. Yes, I am drunk, I am very drunk, but that is no reason why I should permit any one to speak against the unicorn.

SECOND CITIZEN. Let's hear him out. We can do nothing till the sun's up.

SEPTIMUS. Nobody shall speak against the unicorn. No, my friends and poets, nobody. I will hunt it if you will, though it is a dangerous and cross-grained beast. Much virtue has made it cross-grained. I will go with you to the high tablelands of Africa where it lives, and we will there shoot it through the head, but I will not speak against its character, and if any man declares it is not chaste I will fight him, for I affirm that its chastity is equal to its beauty.

THE BIG COUNTRYMAN. He is most monstrously drunk.

SEPTIMUS. No longer drunk but inspired.

SECOND CITIZEN. Go on, go on, we'll never hear the like again.

THE BIG COUNTRYMAN. Come away. I've enough of this we have work to do.

SEPTIMUS. Go away, did you say, and my breast feathers thrust out and my white wings buoyed up with divinity? Ah! but I can see it now you are bent upon going to some lonely place where uninterrupted you can speak against the character of the unicorn, but you shall not, I tell you that you shall not. [*He comes down off the stone and squares up at the crowd which tries to -pass him.*] In the midst of this uncharitable town I will protect that noble, milk-white, flighty beast.

THE BIG COUNTRYMAN. Let me pass.

SEPTIMUS. No, I will not let you pass.

FIRST COUNTRYMAN. Leave him alone.

SECOND COUNTRYMAN. No violence it might bring ill-luck upon us.

[*They try to hold back the Big Countryman.*]

SEPTIMUS. I will oppose your passing to the death. For I will not have it said that there is a smirch, or a blot, upon the most milky whiteness of an heroic brute that bathes by the sound of tabors at the rising of the sun and the rising of the moon, and the rising of the Great Bear, and above all, it shall not be said, whispered, or in any wise published abroad by you that stand there, so to speak, between two washings; for you were doubtless washed when you were born, and, it may be, shall be washed again after you are dead.

[*The Big Countryman knocks him down.*]

FIRST CITIZEN. You have killed him.

THE BIG COUNTRYMAN. Maybe I have, maybe I have not let him lie there. A witch I strangled last Candlemas twelve-month, a witch I will strangle to-day. What do I care for the likes of him?

THIRD CITIZEN. Come round to the east quarter of the town . The basket-makers and the sieve-makers will be out by this.

FOURTH CITIZEN. It is a short march from there to the Castle gate.

[*They go up one of the side streets, but return quickly in confusion and fear.*]

FIRST CITIZEN. Are you sure that you saw him?

SECOND CITIZEN. Who could mistake that horrible old man?

THIRD CITIZEN. I was standing by him when the ghost spoke out of him seven years ago.

FIRST COUNTRYMAN. I never saw him before. He has never been in my district. I don't rightly know what sort he is, but I have heard of him, many a time I have heard of him.

FIRST CITIZEN. His eyes become glassy, and that is the trance growing upon him, and when he is in the trance his soul slips away and a ghost takes its place and speaks out of him—a strange ghost.

THIRD CITIZEN. I was standing by him the last time. 'Get me straw,' said that old man, 'my back itches.' Then all of a sudden he lay down, with his eyes wide open and glassy, and he brayed like a donkey. At that moment the King died and the King's daughter was Queen.

FIRST COUNTRYMAN. They say it is the donkey that carried Christ into Jerusalem and that is why it knows its rightful sovereign. He goes begging about the country and there is no man dare refuse him what he asks.

THE BIG COUNTRYMAN. Then it is certain nobody will take my hand off her throat. I will make my grip tighter. He will be lying down on the straw and he will bray, and when he brays she will be dead.

FIRST COUNTRYMAN. Look! There he is coming over the top of the hill, and the mad look upon him.

SECOND COUNTRYMAN. I wouldn't face him for the world this night. Come round to the market-place, we'll be less afraid in a big place.

THE BIG COUNTRYMAN. I'm not afraid, but I'll go with you till I get my hand on her throat.

[*They all go out but Septimus. Presently Septimus sits up; his head is bleeding. He rubs with his fingers his broken head and looks at the blood on his fingers.*]

SEPTIMUS. Unchristian town! First I am, so to speak, thrown out into the street, and then I am all but murdered; and I drunk, and therefore in need of protection. All creatures are in need of protection at some time or other. Even my wife was once a frail child in need of milk, of smiles, of love, as if in the midst of a flood, in danger of drowning, so to speak.

[*An Old Beggar with long matted hair and beard and in ragged clothes comes in.*]

THE OLD BEGGAR. I want straw.

SEPTIMUS. Happy Tom and Peter of the Purple Pelican have done it all. They are bad, popular poets, and being jealous of my fame, they have stirred up the people. [*He catches sight of the Old Beggar.*] There is a certain medicine which is made by distilling camphor, Peruvian bark, spurge and mandrake, and mixing all with twelve ounces of dissolved pearls and four ounces of the oil of gold; and this medicine is infallible to stop the flow of blood. Have you any of it, old man?

THE OLD BEGGAR. I want straw.

SEPTIMUS. I can see that you have not got it, but no matter, we shall be friends.

THE OLD BEGGAR. I want straw to lie down on.

SEPTIMUS. It is no doubt better that I should bleed to death. For that way, my friend, I shall disgrace Happy Tom and Peter of the Purple Pelican, but it is necessary that I shall die somewhere where my last words can be taken down. I am therefore in need of your support.

[*Having got up he now staggers over to the Old Man and leans upon him.*]

THE OLD BEGGAR. Don't you know who I am aren't you afraid? When something comes inside me, my back itches. Then I must lie down and roll, and then I bray and the crown changes.

SEPTIMUS. Ah! you are inspired. Then we are indeed brothers. Come, I will rest upon your shoulder and we will mount the hill side by side. I will sleep in the Castle of the Queen.

THE OLD BEGGAR. You will give me straw to lie upon?

SEPTIMUS. Asphodels! Yet, indeed, the asphodel is a flower much overrated by the classic authors. Still, if a man has a preference, I say for the asphodel

[*They go out and one hears the voice of Septimus murmuring in the distance about asphodels.*]
[*The First Old Man opens his window and taps with his crutch at the opposite window. The Second Old Man opens his window.*]

FIRST OLD MAN. It is all right now. They are all gone. We can have our talk out.

SECOND OLD MAN. The whole Castle is lit by the dawn now, and it will soon begin to grow brighter in the street.

FIRST OLD MAN. It's time for the Tapster's old dog to come down the street.

SECOND OLD MAN. Yesterday he had a bone in his mouth.

SCENE II

The throne-room in the Castle. Between pillars are gilded openwork doors, except at one side, where there is a large window. The morning light is slanting through the window, making dark shadows among the pillars. As the scene goes on, the light, at first feeble, becomes strong and suffused, and the shadows disappear. Through the openwork doors one can see down long passages, and one of these passages plainly leads into the open air. One can see daylight at the end of it. There is a throne in the centre of the room and a flight of steps that leads to it.

The Prime Minister, an elderly man with an impatient manner and voice, is talking to a group of players, among whom is Nona, a fair, comely, comfortable-looking young woman of perhaps thirty-five; she seems to take the lead.

PRIME MINISTER. I Will not be trifled with. I chose the play myself; I chose "The Tragical History of Noah's Deluge" because when Noah beats his wife to make her go into the Ark everybody understands, everybody is pleased, everybody recognizes the mulish obstinacy of their own wives, sweethearts, sisters. And now, when it is of the greatest importance to the State that everybody should be pleased, the play cannot be given. The leading lady is lost, you say, and there is some unintelligible reason why nobody can take her place; but I know what you are all driving at—you object to the play I have chosen. You want some dull, poetical thing, full of long speeches. I will have that play and no other. The rehearsal must begin at once and the performance take place at noon punctually.

NONA. We have searched all night, sir, and we cannot find her anywhere. She was heard to say that she would drown rather than play a woman older than thirty. Seeing that Noah's wife is a very old woman, we are afraid that she has drowned herself indeed.

[*Decima, a very pretty woman, puts her head out from under the throne where she has been lying hidden.*]

PRIME MINISTER. Nonsense! It is all a conspiracy. Your manager should be here. He is responsible. You can tell him when he does come that if the play is not performed, I will clap him into jail for a year and pitch the rest of you over the border.

NONA. Oh, sir, he couldn't help it. She does whatever she likes.

PRIME MINISTER. Does whatever she likes—I know her sort; would pull the world to pieces to spite her husband or her lover. I know her—a bladder full of dried peas for a brain, a brazen, bragging baggage. Of course he couldn't help it, but what do I care. [*Decima pulls in her head.*] To jail he goes—somebody has got to go to jail. Go and cry her name everywhere. Away with you! Let me hear you cry it out. Call the baggage. Louder. Louder. [*The players go out crying, 'Where are you, Decima?'*] Oh, Adam! why did you fall asleep in the garden? You might have known that while you were lying there helpless, the Old Man in the Sky would play some prank upon you. [*The Queen, who is young, with an ascetic timid face, enters in a badly fitting state dress.*] Ah!

QUEEN. I will show myself to the angry people as you have bidden me. I am almost certain that I am ready for martyrdom. I have prayed all night. Yes, I am almost certain.

PRIME MINISTER. Ah!

QUEEN. I have now attained to the age of my patroness, Holy Saint Octema, when she was martyred at Antioch. You will remember that her unicorn was so pleased at the spectacle of her austerity that he caracoled in his excitement. Thereupon she dropped out of the saddle and was trampled to death under the feet of the mob. Indeed, but for the unicorn, the mob would have killed her long before.

PRIME MINISTER. No, you will not be martyred. I have a plan to settle that. I will stop their anger with a word. Who made that dress?

QUEEN. It was my mother's dress. She wore it at her coronation. I would not have a new one made. I do not deserve new clothes. I am always committing sin.

PRIME MINISTER. Is there sin in an egg that has never been hatched, that has never been warmed, in a chalk egg?

QUEEN. I wish I could resemble Holy Saint Octema in everything.

PRIME MINISTER. What a dress! It is too late now. Nothing can be done. It may appear right to those on the edge of the crowd. The others must be conquered by charm, dignity, royal manner. As for the dress, I must think of some excuse, some explanation. Remember that they have never seen your face, and you will put them in a bad humour if you hang your head in that dumbfounded way.

QUEEN. I wish I could return to my prayers.

PRIME MINISTER. Walk! Permit me to see your Majesty walk. No, no, no. Be more majestic. Ah! If you had known the Queens I have known they had a way with them. Morals of a dragoon, but a way, a way. Give the people some plain image or they will invent one. Put on a kind of eagle look, a vulture look.

QUEEN. There are cobble-stones if I might go barefoot it would be a blessed penance. It was especially the bleeding feet of Saint Octema that gave pleasure to the unicorn.

PRIME MINISTER. Sleep of Adam! Barefoot barefoot, did you say? [*A pause.*] There is not time to take off your shoes and stockings. If you were to look out of the window there, you would see the crowd becoming wickeder every minute. Come! [*He gives his arm to the Queen.*]

QUEEN. You have a plan to stop their anger so that I shall not be martyred?

PRIME MINISTER. My plan will be disclosed before the face of the people and there alone. [*They go out.*]

[*Nona comes in with a bottle of wine and a boiled lobster and lays them on the middle of the floor. She puts her finger on her lip and stands in the doorway towards the back of the stage.*]

DECIMA [*comes cautiously out of her hiding place singing*].
> 'He went away,' my mother sang,
> 'When I was brought to bed.'
> And all the while her needle pulled
> The gold and silver thread.
>
> She pulled the thread and bit the thread
> And made a golden gown,
> She wept because she had dreamt that I
> Was born to wear a crown.

[*She is just reaching her hand for the lobster when Nona comes forward holding out towards her the dress and mask of Noah's wife which she had been carrying over her left arm.*]

NONA. Thank God you are found! [*Getting between her and the lobster.*] No, not until you have put on this dress and mask. I have caught you now and you are not going to hide again.

DECIMA. Very well, when I have had my breakfast.

NONA. Not a mouthful till you are dressed ready for the rehearsal.

DECIMA. Do you know what song I was singing just now?

NONA. It is that song you're always singing. Septimus made it up.

DECIMA. It is the song of the mad singing daughter of a harlot. The only song she had. Her father was a drunken sailor waiting for the full tide, and yet she thought her mother had foretold that she would marry a prince and become a great queen. [*Singing.*]

> 'When she was got,' my mother sang,
> 'I heard a seamew cry,
> I saw a flake of yellow foam
> That dropped upon my thigh.'
>
> How therefore could she help but braid
> The gold upon my hair,
> And dream that I should carry
> The golden top of care.

The moment ago as I lay here I thought I could play a Queen's part, a great Queen's part; the only part in the world I can play is a great Queen's part.

NONA. You play a Queen's part? You that were born in a ditch between two towns and wrapped in a sheet that was stolen from a hedge.

DECIMA. The Queen cannot play at all, but I could play so well. I could bow with my whole body down to my ankles and could be stern when hard looks were in season. Oh, I would know how to put all summer in a look and after that all winter in a voice.

NONA. Low comedy is what you are fit for.

DECIMA. I understood all this in a wink of the eye, and then just when I am saying to myself that I was born to sit up there with soldiers and courtiers, you come shaking in front of me that mask and that dress. I am not to eat my breakfast unless I play an old peaky-chinned, drop-nosed harridan that a foul husband beats with a stick because she won't clamber among the other brutes into his cattle boat. [*She makes a dart at the lobster.*]

NONA. No, no, not a drop, not a mouthful till you have put these on. Remember that if there is no play Septimus must go to prison.

DECIMA. Would they give him dry bread to eat?

NONA. They would.

DECIMA. And water to drink and nothing in the water?

NONA. They would.

DECIMA. And a straw bed?

NONA. They would, and only a little straw maybe.

DECIMA. And iron chains that clanked.

NONA. They would.

DECIMA. And keep him there for a whole week?

NONA. A month maybe.

DECIMA. And he would say to the turnkey, 'I am here because of my beautiful cruel wife, my beautiful flighty wife.'

NONA. He might not, he'd be sober.

DECIMA. But he'd think it and every time he was hungry, every time he was thirsty, every time he felt the hardness of the stone floor, every time he heard the chains clank, he would think it, and every time he thought it I would become more beautiful in his eyes,

NONA. No, he would hate you.

DECIMA. Little do you know what the love of man is. If that Holy Image of the Church where you put all those candles at Easter was pleasant and affable, why did you come home with the skin worn off your two knees?

NONA. [*in tears.*] I understand you cruel, bad woman you won't play the part at all, and all that Septimus may go to prison, and he a great genius that can't take care of himself.

[*Seeing Nona distracted with tears Decima makes a dart and almost gets the lobster.*]

NONA. No, no! Not a mouthful, not a drop. I will break the bottle if you go near it. There is not another woman in the world would treat a man like that and you were sworn to him in Church yes, you were, there is no good denying it. [*Decima makes another dart, but Nona, who is still in tears, puts the lobster in her pocket.*] Leave the food alone; not one mouthful will you get. I have never sworn to a man in Church, but if I did swear I would not treat him like a tinker's donkey before God I would not I was properly brought up; my mother always told me it was no light thing to take a man in Church.

DECIMA. You are in love with my husband.

NONA. Because I don't want to see him jailed you say I am in love with him. Only a woman with no heart would think one can't be sorry for a man without being in love with him. A woman who has never been sorry for anybody, but I won't have him jailed, if you won't play the part I'll play it myself.

DECIMA. When I married him, I made him swear never to play with anybody but me, and well you know it.

NONA. Only this once and in a part nobody can do anything with.

DECIMA. That is the way it begins and all the time you would be saying things the audience couldn't hear.

NONA. Septimus will break his oath and I have learnt the part. Every line of it.

DECIMA. Septimus would not break his oath for anybody in the world.

NONA. There is one person in the world for whom he will break his oath.

DECIMA. What have you in your head now?

NONA. He will break it for me.

DECIMA. You are crazy.

NONA. Maybe I have my secrets.

DECIMA. What are you keeping back? Have you been sitting in corners with Septimus? giving him sympathy because of the bad wife he has and all the while he has sat there to have the pleasure of talking about me?

NONA. You think that you have his every thought because you are a devil.

DECIMA. Because I am a devil I have his every thought. You know how his own song runs. The man speaks first [*singing.*]

> Put off that mask of burning gold
> With emerald eyes,

and then the woman answers—

> Oh no, my dear, you make so bold
> To find if hearts be wild and wise
> And yet not cold.

NONA. His every thought that is a lie. He forgets all about you the moment you're out of his sight.

DECIMA. Then look what I carry under my bodice. This is a poem praising me, all my beauties one after the other eyes, hair, complexion, shape, disposition, mind every-thing. And there are a great many verses to it. And here is a little one he gave me yesterday morning. I had turned him out of bed and he had to lie alone by himself.

NONA. Alone by himself!

DECIMA. And as he lay there alone, unable to sleep, he made it up, wishing that he were blind so as not to be troubled by looking at my beauty. Hear how it goes! [*sings again.*]

> O would that I were an old beggar
> Without a friend on this earth
> But a thieving rascally cur,
> A beggar blind from his birth;
> Or anything else but a man
> Lying alone on a bed
> Remembering a woman's beauty,
> Alone with a crazy head.

NONA. Alone in his bed indeed. I know that long poem, that one with all the verses; I know it to my hurt, though I haven't read a word of it. Four lines in every verse, four beats in every line, and fourteen verses my curse upon it!

DECIMA. [*taking out a manuscript from her bodice*] Yes, fourteen verses. There are numbers to them.

NONA. You have another there ten verses all in fours and threes.

DECIMA. [*looking at another manuscript*] Yes, the verses are in fours and threes. But how do you know all this? I carry them here. They are a secret between him and me, and nobody can see them till they have lain a long while upon my heart.

NONA. They have lain upon your heart, but they were made upon my shoulder. Ay, and down along my spine in the small hours of the morning; so many beats a line, and for every beat a tap of the fingers.

DECIMA. My God!

NONA. That one with the fourteen verses kept me from my sleep two hours, and when the lines were finished he lay upon his back another hour waving one arm in the air, making up the music. I liked him well enough to seem to be asleep through it all, and many another poem too but when he made up that short one you sang he was so pleased that he muttered the words all about his lying alone in his bed thinking of you, and that made me mad. So I said to him, Am I not beautiful? Turn round and look.' Oh, I cut it short, for even I can please a man when there is but one candle. [*She takes a pair of scissors that are hanging round her neck and begins snipping at the dress for Noah's wife.*] And now you know why I can play the part in spite of you and not be driven out. Work upon Septimus if you have a mind for it. Little need I care. I will clip this a trifle and re-stitch it again I have a needle and thread ready.

[*The Stage Manager comes in ringing a bell. He is followed by various players all dressed up in likeness of various beasts.*]

STAGE MANAGER. Put on that mask—get into your clothes. Why are you standing there as if in a trance?

NONA. Decima and I have talked the matter over and we have settled that I am to play the part.

STAGE MANAGER. Do as you please. Thank God it's a part that anybody can play. All you have got to do is to copy an old woman's squeaky voice. We are all here now but Septimus, and we cannot wait for him. I will read the part of Noah. He will be here before we are finished I daresay. We will suppose that the audience is upon this side, and that the Ark is over there with a gangway for the beasts to climb. All you beasts are to crowd up on the prompt side. Lay down Noah's hat and cloak there till Septimus comes. As the first scene is between Noah and the beasts, you can go on with your sewing.

DECIMA. No, I must first be heard. My husband has been spending his nights with Nona, and that is why she sits clipping and stitching with that vainglorious air.

NONA. She made him miserable, she knows every trick of breaking a man's heart—he came to me with his troubles—I seemed to be a comfort to him, and now—why should I deny it?—he is my lover.

DECIMA. I will take the vainglory out of her. I have been a plague to him. Oh, I have been a badger and a weasel and a hedgehog and pole-cat, and all because I was dead sick of him. And, thank God! she has got him and I am free. I threw away a part and I threw away a man—she has picked both up.

STAGE MANAGER. It seems to me that it all concerns you two. It's your business and not ours. I don't see why we should delay the rehearsal.

DECIMA. I will have no rehearsal yet. I'm too happy now that I am free. I must find somebody who will dance with me for a while. Come we must have music. [*She picks up a lute which has been laid down amongst some properties.*] You can't all be claws and hoofs.

STAGE MANAGER. We've only an hour and the whole play to go through.

NONA. Oh, she has taken my scissors, she is only pretending not to care. Look at her! She is mad! Take them away from her! Hold her hand! She is going to kill me or to kill herself. [*To Stage Manager.*] Why don't you interfere? My God! She is going to kill me.

DECIMA. Here, Peter. Play the lute.

[*She begins cutting through the breast feathers of the Swan.*]

NONA. She is doing it all to stop the rehearsal, out of vengeance; and you stand there and do nothing.

STAGE MANAGER. If you have taken her husband, why didn't you keep the news till the play was over? She is going to make them all mad now. I can see that much in her eyes.

DECIMA. Now that I have thrown Septimus into her lap, I will choose a new man. Shall it be you, Turkey-cock? or you, Bullhead?

STAGE MANAGER. There is nothing to be done. It is all your fault. If Septimus can't manage his wife, it's certain that I can't.

[*He sits down helplessly.*]

DECIMA. Dance, Bullhead, dance—no—no—stop. I will not have you for my man, slow on the feet and heavy of build, and that means jealousy, and there is a sort of melancholy in your voice. What a folly that I should find love nothing, and yet through sympathy with that voice should stretch and yawn as if I loved! Dance, Turkey-cock, dance—no, stop. I cannot have you, for my man must be lively on his feet and have a quick eye. I will not have that round eye fixed upon me now that I have sent my mind asleep. Yet what do I care who it is, so that I choose and get done with it? Dance, all dance, and I will choose the best dancer among you. Quick, quick, begin to dance.

[*All dance round Decima.*]

DECIMA [*singing*]. Shall I fancy beast or fowl,
    Queen Pasiphae chose a bull,
    While a passion for a swan
    Made Queen Leda stretch and yawn,
    Wherefore spin ye, whirl ye, dance ye,
    Till Queen Decima's found her fancy.

CHORUS. Wherefore spin ye, whirl ye, dance ye,
    Till Queen Decimals found her fancy.

DECIMA. Spring and straddle, stride and strut,
    Shall I choose a bird or brute?
    Name the feather or the fur
    For my single comforter?

CHORUS. Wherefore spin ye, whirl ye, dance ye,
    Till Queen Decima's found her fancy.

DECIMA. None has found, that found out love,
    Single bird or brute enough;
    Any bird or brute may rest
    An empty head upon my breast.

CHORUS. Wherefore spin ye, whirl ye, dance ye,
Till Queen Decima's found her fancy.

STAGE MANAGER. Stop, stop, here is Septimus.

SEPTIMUS. [*the blood still upon his face and but little soberer.*] Gather about me, for I announce the end of the Christian Era, the coming of a New Dispensation, that of the New Adam, that of the Unicorn; but alas, he is chaste, he hesitates, he hesitates.

STAGE MANAGER. This is not a time for making up speeches for your new play.

SEPTIMUS. His unborn children are but images; we merely play with images.

STAGE MANAGER. Let us get on with the rehearsal.

SEPTIMUS. No; let us prepare to die. The mob is climbing up the hill with pitchforks to stick into our vitals and burning wisps to set the roof on fire.

FIRST PLAYER. [*who has gone to the window*] My God, it's true. There is a great crowd at the bottom of the hill.

SECOND PLAYER. But why should they attack us?

SEPTIMUS. Because we are the servants of the Unicorn.

THIRD PLAYER. [*at window*] My God, they have dung-forks and scythes set on poles and they are coming this way.

[*Many players gather round the window.*]

SEPTIMUS. [*who has found the bottle and is drinking*] Some will die like Cato, some like Cicero, some like Demosthenes, triumphing over death in sonorous eloquence, or, like Petronius Arbiter, will tell witty, scandalous tales; but I will speak, no, I will sing, as if the mob did not exist. I will rail upon the Unicorn for his chastity. I will bid him trample mankind to death and beget a new race. I will even put my railing into rhyme, and all shall run sweetly, sweetly, for, even if they blow up the floor with gunpowder, they are merely the mob.
Upon the round blue eye I rail,
Damnation on the milk-white horn.
A telling sound, a sound to linger in the ear hale, tale, bale, gale—my God, I am even too sober to find a rhyme. [*He drinks and then picks up a lute*]— a tune that my murderers may remember my last words and croon them to their grandchildren.

[*For the next few speeches he is busy making his tune.*]

FIRST PLAYER. The players of this town are jealous. Have we not been chosen before them all, because we are the most famous players in the world? It is they who have stirred up the mob.

SECOND PLAYER. It is of me they are jealous. They know what happened at Xanadu. At the end of that old play The Fall of Troy' Kubla Khan sent for me and said that he would give his kingdom for such a voice, and for such a presence. I stood before him dressed as Agamemnon just as when in a great scene at the end I had reproached Helen for all the misery she had wrought.

FIRST PLAYER. My God, listen to him! Is it not always the comedian who draws the people ? Am I dreaming, and was it not I who was called six times before the curtain? Answer me that—

SECOND PLAYER. What if you were called six dozen times? The players of this town are not jealous because of the crowd's applause. They have that themselves. The unendurable thought, the thought that wrenches their hearts, the thought that puts murder into their minds is that I alone, alone of all the world's players, have looked as an equal into the eyes of Kubla Khan.

STAGE MANAGER. Stop quarrelling with one another and listen to what is happening out there. There is a man making a speech, and the crowd is getting angrier and angrier, and which of you they are jealous of I don't know, but they are all coming this way and maybe they will burn the place down as if it were Troy, and if you will do what I say you will get out of this.

FIRST PLAYER. Must we go dressed like this?

SECOND PLAYER. There is no time to change, and besides should the hill be surrounded, we can gather in some cleft of the rocks where we can be seen only from a distance. They will suppose we are a drove of cattle or a flock of birds.

[*All go out except septimus, Decima, and Nona. Nona is making a bundle of Noah's hat and cloak and other properties. Decima is watching Septimus.*]

SEPTIMUS [*while the players are going out*]. Leave me to die alone? I do not blame you. There is courage in red wine, in white wine, in beer, even in thin beer sold by a blear-eyed potboy in a bankrupt tavern, but there is none in the human heart. When my master the Unicorn bathes by the light of the Great Bear, and to the sound of tabors, even the sweet river-water makes him drunk; but it is cold, it is cold, alas! it is cold.

NONA. I'll pile these upon your back. I shall carry the rest myself and so we shall save all.

[*She begins tying a great bundle of properties on Septimus' back.*]

SEPTIMUS. You are right. I accept the reproach. It is necessary that we who are the last artists—all the rest have gone over to the mob—shall save the images and implements of our art. We must carry into safety the cloak of Noah, the high-crowned hat of Noah, and the golden face of the Almighty, and the horns of Satan.

NONA. Thank God you can still stand upright on your legs.

SEPTIMUS. Tie all upon my back and I will tell you the great secret that came to me at the second mouthful of the bottle. Man is nothing till he is united to an image. Now the Unicorn is both an image and beast; that is why he alone can be the new Adam. When we have put all in safety we will go to the high tablelands of Africa and find where the Unicorn is stabled and sing a marriage song. I will stand before the terrible blue eye.

NONA. There now I have tied them on.

[*She begins making another bundle for herself, but forgets the mask of the sister of Noah. It lies near the Throne.*]

SEPTIMUS. You will make Ionian music—music with its eyes upon that voluptuous Asia—the Dorian scale would but confirm him in his chastity. One Dorian note might undo us, and above all we must be careful not to speak of Delphi. The oracle is chaste.

NONA. Come, let us go.

SEPTIMUS. If we cannot fill him with desire he will deserve death. Even unicorns can be killed. What they dread most in the world is a blow from a knife that has been dipped in the blood of a serpent that died gazing upon an emerald.

[*Nona and Septimus are about to go out, Nona leading Septimus.*]

DECIMA. Stand back, do not dare to move a step.

SEPTIMUS. Beautiful as the unicorn but fierce.

DECIMA. I have locked the gates that we may have a talk.

[*Nona lets the hat of Noah fall in her alarm.*]

SEPTIMUS. That is well, very well. You would talk with me because to-day I am extraordinarily wise.

DECIMA. I will not unlock the gate till I have a promise that you will drive her from the company.

NONA. Do not listen to her; take the key from her.

SEPTIMUS. If I were not her husband I would take the key, but because I am her husband she is terrible. The Unicorn will be terrible when it loves.

NONA. You are afraid.

SEPTIMUS. Could not you yourself take it? She does not love you, therefore she will not be terrible.

NONA. If you are a man at all you will take it.

SEPTIMUS. I am more than a man, I am extraordinarily wise. I will take the key.

DECIMA. If you come a step nearer I will shove the key through the grating of the door.

NONA. [*pulling him back*] Don't go near her; if she shoves it through the door we shall not be able to escape. The crowd will find us and murder us.

DECIMA. I will unlock this gate when you have taken an oath to drive her from the company, an oath never to speak with her or look at her again, a terrible oath.

SEPTIMUS. You are jealous; it is very wrong to be jealous. An ordinary man would be lost—even I am not yet wise enough. [*Drinks again.*] Now all is plain.

DECIMA. You have been unfaithful to me.

SEPTIMUS. I am only unfaithful when I am sober. Never trust a sober man. All the world over they are unfaithful. Never trust a man who has not bathed by the light of the Great Bear. I warn you against all sober men from the bottom of my heart. I am extraordinarily wise.

NONA. Promise, if it is only an oath she wants. Take whatever oath she bids you. If you delay we shall all be murdered.

SEPTIMUS. I can see your meaning. You would explain to me that an oath can be broken, more especially an oath under compulsion, but no, I say to you, no, I say to you, certainly not. Am I a rascally sober man, such a man as I have warned you against? Shall I be foresworn before the very eyes of Delphi, so to speak, before the very eyes of that cold, rocky oracle? What I promise I perform, therefore, my little darling, I will not promise anything at all.

DECIMA. Then we shall wait here. They will come in there and there, they will carry dung-forks with burning wisps. They will put the burning wisps into the roof and we shall be burnt.

SEPTIMUS. I shall die railing upon that beast. The Christian era has come to an end, but because of the machinations of Delphi he will not become the new Adam.

DECIMA. I shall be avenged. She starved me, but I shall have killed her.

NONA. [*who has crept behind Decima and snatched the key*] I have it, I have it!

[*Decima tries to take the key again but Septimus holds her.*]

SEPTIMUS. Because I am an unforesworn man I am strong: a violent virginal creature, that is how it is put in "The Great Beastery of Paris."

DECIMA. Go, then. I shall stay here and die.

NONA. Let us go. A half hour since she offered herself to every man in the company.

DECIMA. If you would be faithful to me, Septimus, I would not let a man of them touch me.

SEPTIMUS. Flighty, but beautiful.

NONA. She is a bad woman.

[*Nona runs out.*]

SEPTIMUS. A beautiful, bad, flighty woman I will follow, but follow slowly. I will take with me this noble hat. [*He picks up Noah's hat with difficulty.*] I will save the noble, high-crowned hat of Noah. I will carry it thus with dignity. I will go slowly that they may see I am not afraid. [*singing.*]

> Upon the round blue eye I rail
> Damnation on the milk-white horn.

But not one word of Delphi. I am extraordinarily wise. [*He goes.*]

DECIMA. Betrayed, betrayed, and for a nobody. For a woman that a man can shake and twist like so much tallow. A woman that till now never looked higher than a prompter or a property man. [*The Old Beggar comes in.*] Have you come to kill me, old man?

OLD BEGGAR. I am looking for straw. I must soon lie down and roll, and where will I get straw to roll on? I went round to the kitchen and 'Go away' they said. They made the sign of the cross as if it were a devil that puts me rolling.

DECIMA. When will the mob come to kill me?

OLD BEGGAR. Kill you? It is not you they are going to kill. It's the itching in my back that drags them hither, for when I bray like a donkey, the crown changes.

DECIMA. The crown? So it is the Queen they are going to kill.

OLD BEGGAR. But, my dear, she can't die till I roll and bray, and I will whisper to you what it is that rolls. It is the donkey that carried Christ into Jerusalem, and that is why he is so proud; and that is why he knows the hour when there is to be a new King or a new Queen.

DECIMA. Are you weary of the world, old man?

OLD BEGGAR. Yes, yes, because when I roll and bray I am asleep. I know nothing about it, and that is a great pity. I remember nothing but the itching in my back. But I must stop talking and find some straw.

DECIMA. [*picking up the scissors*] Old man, I am going to drive this into my heart.

OLD BEGGAR. No, no; don't do that. You don't know what you will be put to when you are dead, into whose gullet you will be put to sing or to bray. You have a look of a foretelling sort. Who knows but you might be put to foretell the death of kings; and bear in mind I will have no rivals, I could not endure a rival.

DECIMA. I have been betrayed by a man, I have been made a mockery of. Do those who are dead, old man, make love and do they find good lovers?

OLD BEGGAR. I will whisper you another secret. People talk, but I have never known of anything to come from there but an old jackass. Maybe there is nothing else. Who knows but he has the whole place to himself. But there, my back is beginning to itch, and I have not yet found any straw.

[*He goes out. Decima leans the scissors upon the arm of the throne and is about to press herself upon them when the Queen enters.*]

QUEEN. [*stopping her*] No, no, that would be a great sin.

DECIMA. Your Majesty!

QUEEN. I thought I would like to die a martyr, but that would be different, that would be to die for God's glory. The Holy Saint Octema was a martyr.

DECIMA. I am very unhappy.

QUEEN. I, too, am very unhappy. When I saw the great angry crowd and knew that they wished to kill me, though I had wanted to be a martyr, I was afraid and ran away.

DECIMA. I would not have run away. Oh no, but it is hard to drive a knife into one's own flesh.

QUEEN. In a moment they will have command they will beat in the door, and how shall I escape them?

DECIMA. If they could mistake me for you, you would escape.

QUEEN. I could not let another die instead of me. That would be very wrong.

DECIMA. Oh, your Majesty, I shall die whatever you do, and if only I could wear that gold brocade and those gold slippers for one moment, it would not be so hard to die.

QUEEN. They say that those who die to save a rightful sovereign show great virtue.

DECIMA. Quick! the dress.

QUEEN. If you killed yourself your soul would be lost, and now you will be sure of heaven.

DECIMA. Quick, I hear them coming.

[*Decima puts on the Queen's robe of state and her slippers. Underneath her robe of state the Queen wears some kind of nun-like dress.*]

[*The following speech is spoken by the Queen while she is helping Decima to fasten the dress and the slippers.*]

QUEEN. Was it love? [*Decima nods.*] Oh, that is a great sin. I have never known love. Of all things, that is what I have had most fear of. Saint Octema shut herself up in a tower on a mountain because she was loved by a beautiful prince. I was afraid it would come in at the eye and seize upon me in a moment. I am not naturally good, and they say people will do anything for love, there is so much sweetness in it. Even Saint Octema was afraid of it. But you will escape all that and go up to God as a pure virgin. [*The change is now complete.*] Goodbye, I know how I can slip away. There is a convent that will take me in. It is not a tower, it is only a convent, but I have long wanted to go there to lose my name and disappear. Sit down upon the throne and turn your face away. If you do not turn your face away, you will be afraid. [*The Queen goes out.*]

[*Decima is seated upon the throne. A great crowd gathers outside the gates. A Bishop enters.*]

BISHOP. Your loyal people, your Majesty, offer you their homage. I bow before you in their name. Your royal will has spoken by the mouth of the Prime Minister—has filled them with gratitude. All misunderstandings are at an end, all has been settled by your condescension in bestowing your royal hand upon the Prime Minister. [*To crowd.*] Her Majesty, who has hitherto shut herself away from all men's eyes that she might pray for this kingdom undisturbed, will henceforth show herself to her people. [*To Player Queen.*] So beautiful a queen need never fear the disobedience of her people [*shouts from crowd of 'Never.'*]

PRIME MINISTER. [*entering hurriedly*] I will explain all, your Majesty—there was nothing else to be done—This Bishop has been summoned to unite us [*seeing the Queen*]; but, sleep of Adam!—this who is this?

DECIMA. Your emotion is too great for words. Do not try to speak.

PRIME MINISTER. This—this…!

DECIMA. [*standing up*] I am Queen. I know what it is to be queen. If I were to say to you I had an enemy you would kill him you would tear him in pieces. [*Shouts: 'We would kill him', 'We would tear him in Pieces', etc.*] But I do not bid you kill any one—I bid you obey my husband when I have raised him to the throne. He is not of royal blood, but I choose to raise him to the throne. That is my will. Show me that you will obey him so long as I bid you to obey. [*Great cheering.*]

[*Septimus, who has been standing among the crowd, comes forward and takes the Prime Minister by the sleeve. Various persons kiss the hand of the supposed Queen.*]

SEPTIMUS. My Lord, that is not the queen; that is my bad wife. [*Decima looks at them.*]

PRIME MINISTER. Did you see that? Did you see the devil in her eye. They are mad after her pretty face, and she knows it. They would not believe a word I say; there is nothing to be done till they cool.

DECIMA. Are all here my faithful servants?

BISHOP. All, your Majesty.

DECIMA. All?

PRIME MINISTER [*bowing low*]. All, your Majesty.

DECIMA [*singing*].

> She pulled the thread, and bit the thread
> And made a golden gown.

Hand me that plate of lobster and that bottle of wine. While I am eating I will have a good look at my new man.

[*The plate and bottle of wine are handed to her. The bray of a donkey is heard and the Old Beggar is dragged in.*]

BISHOP. At last we have found this impostor out. He has been accepted by the whole nation as if he were the Voice of God. As if the crown could not be settled firmly on any head without his help. It's plain that he has been in league with the conspirators, and believed that your Majesty had been killed. He is keeping it up still. Look at his glassy eye. But his madman airs won't help him now.

PRIME MINISTER. Carry him to prison, we will hang him in the morning. [*shaking Septimus*] Do you understand that there has been a miracle, that God or the Fiend has spoken, and that the crown is on her head for good, that fate has brayed on that man's lips. [*Aloud.*] We will hang him in the morning.

SEPTIMUS. She is my wife.

PRIME MINISTER. The crown has changed and there is no help for it. Sleep of Adam, I must have that woman for wife. The Oracle has settled that.

SEPTIMUS. She is my wife, she is my bad, flighty wife.

PRIME MINISTER. Seize this man. He has been whispering slanders against her Majesty. Cast him beyond the borders of the kingdom, and his players after him.

DECIMA. He must not return upon pain of death. He has wronged me, and I will never look upon his face again.

PRIME MINISTER. Away with him.

DECIMA. My good name is dearer than my life, but I will see the players before they go.

PRIME MINISTER. Sleep of Adam! What has she got into her head? Fetch the players.

DECIMA. [*Picking up the mask of the sister of Noah.*] My loyal subjects must forgive me if I hide my face—it is not yet used to the light of day, it is a modest face. I will be much happier if His Holiness will help me to tie the mask.

PRIME MINISTER. The players come.

[*Enter Players, who all bow to the new Queen.*]

DECIMA. They had some play they were to perform, but I will make them dance instead, and after that they must be richly rewarded.

PRIME MINISTER. It shall be as you will.

DECIMA. You are banished and must not return upon pain of death, and yet not one of you shall be poorer because banished. That I promise. But you have lost one thing that I will not restore. A woman player has left you. Do not mourn her. She was a bad, headstrong, cruel woman and seeks destruction somewhere and with some man she knows nothing of; such a woman, they tell me that this mask would well become, this foolish, smiling face! Come, dance.

[*They dance, and at certain moments she cries 'Good-bye, good-bye' or else 'Farewell'. And she throws them money.*]

THE END